Patterns and Formulas for Phonetic Groups in Mandarin Chinese Characters Volume 59

by

Stephen M Kraemer

In looking at Chinese characters in Mandarin, many phonetic compound/phonetic element character pairs or groups exhibit certain patterns. These phonetic patterns are based on the syllable structure of Modern Standard Mandarin, namely the syllable being composed of an initial, final, and tone. The final portion of the syllable is further composed of the rime (nuclear vowel + ending)(ending being a vowel or consonant).

(For vowel and consonant features in Mandarin, see Kratochvil 1968).

As part of the phonetic patterns given here, formulas for the arrangement of character segments (vowels and consonants) will include one or more of the six pinyin vowels and two final consonants as follows:

V1 = i

V2 = e

V3 = a

V4 = u [u]; V4 = o [u]*

V5 = ü

V6 = o [o]

C1 = n

C2 = ng

*Note: In the pinyin finals "ao," "iao," "ong," "iong," the pinyin letter "o" represents V4, the high, back rounded vowel [u]. In the pinyin finals "o," "ou," "iou{iu}," "uo," the pinyin letter "o" represents V6, the mid, back rounded vowel [o].)

In this study, three groups of phonetic characters in Mandarin will be shown. These include the 那 (nà, nèi, nā) group, where all characters share the common phonetic element 那 (nà, nèi, nā); the 内(nèi) group, where all characters share the common phonetic element 内 (nèi); and the 乃 (nǎi) group, where all characters share the common phonetic element 乃(nǎi).

Providing information about the phonetic patterns of Chinese characters may serve to help the student of Chinese to recognize the phonetic relationship among many characters in Mandarin. Teachers of Chinese may also find this book useful in seeing how phonetic elements can be arranged to show how they share certain features of their pronunciation with other characters.

Character pronunciations are given in pinyin and are taken from Zhou You-guang (1980), based on Xin Hua Zidian (1971). Where the phonetic element character pronunciation is not found in either Zhou You-guang (1980) or Xin Hua Zidian (1971), it is taken from Handian (2004 – 2015).

那(nà, nèi, nā)

那(nà)

娜(nà)

Phonetic Pattern:

Voiced Alveolar (n)

Totally Perfect

(nà)

(na)

Alveolar V3

(V3 = a)

那(nā)

娜(nà)

Phonetic Pattern:
Voiced Alveolar (n)
Segment Perfect
(na)

(na)

Alveolar V3

(V3 = a)

那(nà, nā)

哪(nǎ)

哪(na)

Phonetic Pattern:
Voiced Alveolar (n)
Segment Perfect
(na)

(na)
Alveolar V3
(V3 = a)

那(nà, nā)

哪(něi)

Phonetic Pattern:

Voiced Alveolar (n) Initial Perfect (n) All Unrounded Vowel Finals (a/ei)

(na/nei)
Alveolar V3 +
Alveolar V2V1
(V3 = a)(V2 = e)(V1 = i)

那(nà, nā)

哪(né)

Phonetic Pattern:
Voiced Alveolar (n)
Initial Perfect (n)
All Non-High, Back, Unrounded Single Vowel Finals
(a/e) [ɑ] [ɤ]

(na/ne)

Alveolar V3 +

Alveolar V2

(V3 = a)(V2 = e)

那(nà, nā)

娜(nuó)

挪(nuó)

Phonetic Pattern:

Voiced Alveolar (n)
Initial Perfect (n)
All Back Vowel Finals
(a/uo) [ɑ] [uo]

(na/nuo)
Alveolar V3 +
Alveolar V4V6
(V3 = a)(V4 = u)(V6 = o)

那(nèi)

哪(něi)

Phonetic Pattern:

Voiced Alveolar (n)
Segment Perfect
(nei)

(nei)
Alveolar V2V1
(V2 = e)(V1 = i)

那(nèi)

哪(né)

Phonetic Pattern:

Voiced Alveolar (n)
Initial Perfect (n)
All Non-Low, Unrounded
Vowel Finals (ei/e)
Mid, Unrounded
First Vowel (e)

(nei/ne)
Alveolar V2V1 +
Alveolar V2
(V2 = e)(V1 = i)

那(nèi)

娜(nà)

Phonetic Pattern:

Voiced Alveolar (n)
Initial Perfect (n)
All Unrounded Vowel
Finals (ei/a)
Tone Perfect (Tone 4)

(nei/na)
Alveolar V2V1 +
Alveolar V3
(V2 = e)(V1 = i)(V3 = a)

那(nèi)

哪(nǎ)
哪(na)

Phonetic Pattern:
Voiced Alveolar (n) Initial Perfect (n) All Unrounded Vowel Finals (ei/a)

(nei/na)

Alveolar V2V1 +

Alveolar V3

(V2 = e)(V1 = i)(V3 = a)

那(nèi)

娜(nuó)
挪(nuó)

Phonetic Pattern:

Voiced Alveolar (n)
Initial Perfect (n)
All Non-Low (Diphthong)
Vowel Finals (ei/uo)
Mid Vowel (e/o)

(nei/nuo)
Alveolar V2V1 +
Alveolar V4V6
(V2 = e)(V1 = i)
(V4 = u)(V6 = o)

内(nèi)

内(nèi)

讷(nè)

Phonetic Pattern:

Voiced Alveolar (n)
Initial Perfect (n)
All Non-Low, Unrounded
Vowel Finals (ei/e)
Mid, Unrounded
First Vowel (e)
Tone Perfect (Tone 4)

(nei/ne)
Alveolar V2V1 +
Alveolar V2
(V2 = e)(V1 = i)

内(nèi)

纳(nà)
钠(nà)
呐(nà)
肭(nà)
衲(nà)

Phonetic Pattern:

Voiced Alveolar (n)
Initial Perfect (n)
All Unrounded Vowel
Finals (ei/a)
Tone Perfect (Tone 4)

(nei/na)
Alveolar V2V1 +
Alveolar V3
(V2 = e)(V1 = i)(V3 = a)

内(nèi)

芮(ruì)
蚋(ruì)
枘(ruì)
汭(ruì)

Phonetic Pattern:
Voiced Alveolar/Voiced Retroflex (n/r) Rime-Tone Perfect (èi)

(nei/rui)

Alveolar V2V1 +

Retroflex V4V2V1

(V2 = e)(V1 = i)(V4 = u)

(ui = uei)

乃(nǎi)

乃(nǎi)

奶(nǎi)
艿(nǎi)
氖(nǎi)

Phonetic Pattern:
Voiced Alveolar (n)
Totally Perfect
(nǎi)

(nai)
Alveolar V3V1
(V3 = a)(V1 = i)

乃(nǎi)

鼐(nài)

Phonetic Pattern:

Voiced Alveolar (n)
Segment Perfect
(nai)

(nai)
Alveolar V3V1
(V3 = a)(V1 = i)

乃(nǎi)

扔(rēng)
仍(réng)
礽(réng)

Phonetic Pattern:
Voiced Alveolar/Voiced Retroflex (n/r) Unrounded Vowels (ai/e)

(nai/reng)
Alveolar V3V1 +
Retroflex V2C2
(V3 = a)(V1 = i)
(V2 = e)(C2 = ng)

References

Cheng, C.C. (1973). *A synchronic phonology of Mandarin Chinese*. The Hague: Mouton.

Handian [<汉典>, ‘字典’]. Online Chinese dictionary. (2004 – 2015). http://www.zdic.net

Kraemer, Stephen M. (1980). *Potentially pedagogically useful phonetics in the Chinese script: Their identification and characterization*. Doctoral dissertation. Rutgers University.

Kraemer, Stephen M. (1991a). *Sound clues in Mandarin character phonetic series*. Retrieved from https://scholarsbank.uoregon.edu/xmlui/handle/1794/4943

Kraemer, Stephen M. (1991b). *Levels of phonological regularity in the Chinese writing system*. Retrieved from https://scholarsbank.uoregon.edu/xmlui/handle/1794/8133

Kraemer, Stephen M. (2017). *Let's Learn Mandarin Phonics*. CreateSpace Independent Publishing Platform.

Kraemer, Stephen M. (2017). *Let's Learn Mandarin Phonics-2*. CreateSpace Independent Publishing Platform.

Kraemer, Stephen M. (2018a). *Let's Learn Mandarin Phonics-3. Rime Clue, Rime-Tone Clue, Ending Clue, Ending-Tone Clue Phonetic Patterns of Common Chinese Characters.* CreateSpace Independent Publishing Platform.

Kraemer, Stephen M. (2018b). *Let's Learn Mandarin Phonics-4. Initial Clue, Initial-Tone Clue, Tone-Clue and Related Phonetic Patterns of Common Chinese Characters.* CreateSpace Independent Publishing Platform.

Kraemer, Stephen M. (2018c). *Let's Learn Mandarin Phonics-5. Vowel Phonetic Clues for Common Chinese Characters.* CreateSpace Independent Publishing Platform.

Kraemer, Stephen M. (2018d). *Phonetic Clues for Learning Common Chinese Characters.* CreateSpace Independent Publishing Platform.

Kraemer, Stephen M. (2018e). *A Phonetic Guide to Learning Chinese Characters.* CreateSpace Independent Publishing Platform.

Kraemer, Stephen M.(2020). *Phonetic Patterns in Mandarin Chinese Characters: Pinyin "ng" Ending Finals with Unrounded Vowels*. Independent Publishing Platform.

Kraemer, Stephen M.(2020a). *Phonetic Patterns in Mandarin Chinese Characters: Pinyin "n/ng" Ending Finals with Unrounded Vowels*. Independent Publishing Platform.

Kraemer, Stephen M.(2020b). *Phonetic Patterns in Mandarin Chinese Characters: V/VC1 Finals.* Independent Publishing Platform.

Kraemer, Stephen M.(2020c). *Phonetic Patterns in Mandarin Chinese Characters: VC1 Finals with Unrounded Vowels.* Independent Publishing Platform.

Kraemer, Stephen M.(2020d). *Phonetic Patterns in Mandarin Chinese Characters: V Finals with a Rounded Medial Vowel Plus Unrounded V*. Independent Publishing Platform.

Kraemer, Stephen M.(2020e). *Phonetic Patterns in Mandarin Chinese Characters: V Finals with a Rounded Ending Vowel Plus Unrounded V*. Independent Publishing Platform.

Kraemer, Stephen M.(2020f). *Phonetic Patterns in Mandarin Chinese Characters: Labial/Velar Initials and Pinyin "m"/ "w"*. Independent Publishing Platform.

Kraemer, Stephen M.(2020g). *Phonetic Patterns in Mandarin Chinese Characters: Velar/Retroflex Initials*. Independent Publishing Platform.

Kraemer, Stephen M.(2020h). *Phonetic Patterns in Mandarin Chinese Characters: Velar/Alveolar Initials*. Independent Publishing Platform.

Kraemer, Stephen M.(2020i). *Phonetic Patterns in Mandarin Chinese Characters: Palatal Initials*. Independent Publishing Platform.

Kraemer, Stephen M.(2020j). *Phonetic Patterns in Chinese Characters: Pinyin "a/e" Variation in Mandarin*. Independent Publishing Platform.

Kraemer, Stephen M.(2020k). *Phonetic Groups in Chinese Characters: All Unrounded Vowel Finals in Mandarin*. Independent Publishing Platform.

Kraemer, Stephen M.(2020l). *Phonetic Groups in Chinese Characters: All Unrounded Vowel Finals in Mandarin Volume 2*. Independent Publishing Platform.

Kraemer, Stephen M.(2020m). *Phonetic Groups in Chinese Characters: All Unrounded Vowel Finals in Mandarin Volume 3*. Independent Publishing Platform.

Kraemer, Stephen M.(2020n). *Phonetic Groups in Chinese Characters: All Vowel Finals in Mandarin*. Independent Publishing Platform.

Kraemer, Stephen M.(2020o). *Phonetic Groups in Chinese Characters: All Vowel Finals in Mandarin Volume 2*. Independent Publishing Platform.

Kraemer, Stephen M.(2020p). *Phonetic Groups in Chinese Characters: All Vowel Finals in Mandarin Volume 3*. Independent Publishing Platform.

Kraemer, Stephen M.(2020q). *Phonetic Patterns in Mandarin Chinese Characters: Final Perfect with Palatal j/x, q/x Initials*. Independent Publishing Platform.

Kraemer, Stephen M.(2020r). *Phonetic Groups in Chinese Characters: All Unrounded Vowel Finals in Mandarin Volume 4*. Independent Publishing Platform.

Kraemer, Stephen M.(2020s). *Phonetic Groups in Chinese Characters: All Vowel Finals in Mandarin Volume 4*. Independent Publishing Platform.

Kraemer, Stephen M.(2020t). *Phonetic Patterns in Mandarin Chinese Characters: Final Perfect with Palatal j/q Initials*. Independent Publishing Platform.

Kraemer, Stephen M.(2020u). *Phonetic Patterns in Mandarin Chinese Characters: Final Perfect with Palatal Initials*. Independent Publishing Platform.

Kraemer, Stephen M.(2020v). *Phonetic Components for Meaning in Mandarin Chinese Characters*. Independent Publishing Platform.

Kraemer, Stephen M.(2020w). *Phonetic Components for Meaning in Mandarin Chinese Characters Volume* 2. Independent Publishing Platform.

Kraemer, Stephen M.(2020x). *Phonetic Components for Meaning in Mandarin Chinese Characters Volume 3*. Independent Publishing Platform.

Kraemer, Stephen M.(2020y). *Phonetic Components for Meaning in Mandarin Chinese Characters Volume 4*. Independent Publishing Platform.

Kraemer, Stephen M.(2020z). *Phonetic Components for Meaning in Mandarin Chinese Characters Volume 5*. Independent Publishing Platform.

Kraemer, Stephen M.(2020aa). *Phonetic Components for Meaning in Mandarin Chinese Characters Volume 6*. Independent Publishing Platform.

Kraemer, Stephen M.(2020ab). *Phonetic Components for Meaning in Mandarin Chinese Characters Volume 7*. Independent Publishing Platform.

Kraemer, Stephen M.(2020ac). *Semantic Compounds in Mandarin Chinese Characters*. Independent Publishing Platform.

Kraemer, Stephen M.(2020ad). *Patterns and Formulas for Phonetic Groups in Mandarin Chinese Characters*. Independent Publishing Platform.

Kraemer, Stephen M.(2020ae). *Patterns and Formulas for Phonetic Groups in Mandarin Chinese Characters Volume 2*. Independent Publishing Platform.

Kraemer, Stephen M.(2020af). *Patterns and Formulas for Phonetic Groups in Mandarin Chinese Characters Volume 3*. Independent Publishing Platform.

Kraemer, Stephen M.(2020ag). *Patterns and Formulas for Phonetic Groups in Mandarin Chinese Characters Volume 4*. Independent Publishing Platform.

Kraemer, Stephen M.(2020ah). *Patterns and Formulas for Phonetic Groups in Mandarin Chinese Characters Volume 5.* Independent Publishing Platform.

Kraemer, Stephen M.(2020ai). *Patterns and Formulas for Phonetic Groups in Mandarin Chinese Characters Volume 6.* Independent Publishing Platform.

Kraemer, Stephen M.(2020aj). *Patterns and Formulas for Phonetic Groups in Mandarin Chinese Characters Volume 7.* Independent Publishing Platform.

Kraemer, Stephen M.(2020ak). *Patterns and Formulas for Phonetic Groups in Mandarin Chinese Characters Volume 8.* Independent Publishing Platform.

Kraemer, Stephen M.(2020al). *Patterns and Formulas for Phonetic Groups in Mandarin Chinese Characters Volume 9.* Independent Publishing Platform.

Kraemer, Stephen M.(2020am). *Patterns and Formulas for Phonetic Groups in Mandarin Chinese Characters Volume 10.* Independent Publishing Platform.

Kraemer, Stephen M.(2020an). *Patterns and Formulas for Phonetic Groups in Mandarin Chinese Characters Volume 11.* Independent Publishing Platform.

Kraemer, Stephen M.(2020ao). *Patterns and Formulas for Phonetic Groups in Mandarin Chinese Characters Volume 12.* Independent Publishing Platform.

Kraemer, Stephen M.(2020ap). *Patterns and Formulas for Phonetic Groups in Mandarin Chinese Characters Volume 14*. Independent Publishing Platform.

Kraemer, Stephen M.(2020aq). *Patterns and Formulas for Phonetic Groups in Mandarin Chinese Characters Volume 15*. Independent Publishing Platform.

Kraemer, Stephen M.(2020ar). *Patterns and Formulas for Phonetic Groups in Mandarin Chinese Characters Volume 16.* Independent Publishing Platform.

Kraemer, Stephen M.(2020as). *Patterns and Formulas for Phonetic Groups in Mandarin Chinese Characters Volume 17.* Independent Publishing Platform.

Kraemer, Stephen M.(2020at). *Patterns and Formulas for Phonetic Groups in Mandarin Chinese Characters Volume 18*. Independent Publishing Platform.

Kraemer, Stephen M.(2020au). *Patterns and Formulas for Phonetic Groups in Mandarin Chinese Characters Volume 19*. Independent Publishing Platform.

Kraemer, Stephen M.(2020av). *Patterns and Formulas for Phonetic Groups in Mandarin Chinese Characters Volume 20.* Independent Publishing Platform.

Kraemer, Stephen M.(2020aw). *Patterns and Formulas for Phonetic Groups in Mandarin Chinese Characters Volume 21.* Independent Publishing Platform.

Kraemer, Stephen M.(2020ax). *Patterns and Formulas for Phonetic Groups in Mandarin Chinese Characters Volume 22.* Independent Publishing Platform.

Kraemer, Stephen M.(2020ay). *Patterns and Formulas for Phonetic Groups in Mandarin Chinese Characters Volume 23.* Independent Publishing Platform.

Kraemer, Stephen M.(2020az). *Patterns and Formulas for Phonetic Groups in Mandarin Chinese Characters Volume 24.* Independent Publishing Platform.

Kraemer, Stephen M.(2020aaa). *Patterns and Formulas for Phonetic Groups in Mandarin Chinese Characters Volume 25.* Independent Publishing Platform.

Kraemer, Stephen M.(2020aab). *Patterns and Formulas for Phonetic Groups in Mandarin Chinese Characters Volume 26.* Independent Publishing Platform.

Kraemer, Stephen M.(2020aac). *Patterns and Formulas for Phonetic Groups in Mandarin Chinese Characters Volume 27.* Independent Publishing Platform.

Kraemer, Stephen M.(2020aad). *Patterns and Formulas for Phonetic Groups in Mandarin Chinese Characters Volume 28*. Independent Publishing Platform.

Kraemer, Stephen M.(2020aae). *Patterns and Formulas for Phonetic Groups in Mandarin Chinese Characters Volume 29*. Independent Publishing Platform.

Kraemer, Stephen M.(2020aaf). *Patterns and Formulas for Phonetic Groups in Mandarin Chinese Characters Volume 30.* Independent Publishing Platform.

Kraemer, Stephen M.(2020aag). *Patterns and Formulas for Phonetic Groups in Mandarin Chinese Characters Volume 31.* Independent Publishing Platform.

Kraemer, Stephen M.(2020aah). *Patterns and Formulas for Phonetic Groups in Mandarin Chinese Characters Volume 32.* Independent Publishing Platform.

Kraemer, Stephen M.(2020aai). *Patterns and Formulas for Phonetic Groups in Mandarin Chinese Characters Volume 33.* Independent Publishing Platform.

Kraemer, Stephen M.(2020aaj). *Patterns and Formulas for Phonetic Groups in Mandarin Chinese Characters Volume 34*. Independent Publishing Platform.

Kraemer, Stephen M.(2020aak). *Patterns and Formulas for Phonetic Groups in Mandarin Chinese Characters Volume 35*. Independent Publishing Platform.

Kraemer, Stephen M.(2020aal). *Patterns and Formulas for Phonetic Groups in Mandarin Chinese Characters Volume 36.* Independent Publishing Platform.

Kraemer, Stephen M.(2020aam). *Patterns and Formulas for Phonetic Groups in Mandarin Chinese Characters Volume 37.* Independent Publishing Platform.

Kraemer, Stephen M.(2020aan). *Patterns and Formulas for Phonetic Groups in Mandarin Chinese Characters Volume 38.* Independent Publishing Platform.

Kraemer, Stephen M.(2020aao). *Patterns and Formulas for Phonetic Groups in Mandarin Chinese Characters Volume 39.* Independent Publishing Platform.

Kraemer, Stephen M.(2020aap). *Patterns and Formulas for Phonetic Groups in Mandarin Chinese Characters Volume 40.* Independent Publishing Platform.

Kraemer, Stephen M.(2020aaq). *Patterns and Formulas for Phonetic Groups in Mandarin Chinese Characters Volume 41.* Independent Publishing Platform.

Kraemer, Stephen M.(2020aar). *Patterns and Formulas for Phonetic Groups in Mandarin Chinese Characters Volume 42.* Independent Publishing Platform.

Kraemer, Stephen M.(2020aas). *Patterns and Formulas for Phonetic Groups in Mandarin Chinese Characters Volume 43.* Independent Publishing Platform.

Kraemer, Stephen M.(2020aat). *Patterns and Formulas for Phonetic Groups in Mandarin Chinese Characters Volume 44.* Independent Publishing Platform.

Kraemer, Stephen M.(2020aau). *Patterns and Formulas for Phonetic Groups in Mandarin Chinese Characters Volume 45.* Independent Publishing Platform.

Kraemer, Stephen M.(2020aav). *Patterns and Formulas for Phonetic Groups in Mandarin Chinese Characters Volume 46.* Independent Publishing Platform.

Kraemer, Stephen M.(2020aaw). *Patterns and Formulas for Phonetic Groups in Mandarin Chinese Characters Volume 47.* Independent Publishing Platform.

Kraemer, Stephen M.(2020aax). *Patterns and Formulas for Phonetic Groups in Mandarin Chinese Characters Volume 48.* Independent Publishing Platform.

Kraemer, Stephen M.(2020aay). *Patterns and Formulas for Phonetic Groups in Mandarin Chinese Characters Volume 49.* Independent Publishing Platform.

Kraemer, Stephen M.(2020aaz). *Patterns and Formulas for Phonetic Groups in Mandarin Chinese Characters Volume 50.* Independent Publishing Platform.

Kraemer, Stephen M.(2020aaaa). *Patterns and Formulas for Phonetic Groups in Mandarin Chinese Characters Volume 51.* Independent Publishing Platform.

Kraemer, Stephen M.(2020aaab). *Patterns and Formulas for Phonetic Groups in Mandarin Chinese Characters Volume 52.* Independent Publishing Platform.

Kraemer, Stephen M.(2020aaac). *Patterns and Formulas for Phonetic Groups in Mandarin Chinese Characters Volume 53.* Independent Publishing Platform.

Kraemer, Stephen M.(2020aaad). *Patterns and Formulas for Phonetic Groups in Mandarin Chinese Characters Volume 54*. Independent Publishing Platform.

Kraemer, Stephen M.(2020aaae). *Patterns and Formulas for Phonetic Groups in Mandarin Chinese Characters Volume 55*. Independent Publishing Platform.

Kraemer, Stephen M.(2020aaaf). *Patterns and Formulas for Phonetic Groups in Mandarin Chinese Characters Volume 56.* Independent Publishing Platform.

Kraemer, Stephen M.(2020aaag). *Patterns and Formulas for Phonetic Groups in Mandarin Chinese Characters Volume 57.* Independent Publishing Platform.

Kraemer, Stephen M.(2021). *Patterns and Formulas for Phonetic Groups in Mandarin Chinese Characters Volume 58.* Independent Publishing Platform.

Kratochvil, Paul. (1968). *The Chinese language today: Features of an emerging standard*. London: Hutchinson & Co., Ltd.

Xinhua zidian (New China dictionary). (1971). Beijing: Shangwu Yinshuguan. [<新华字典>, 1971，北京：商务印书馆.]

Zhou, Youguang. (1980). *Hanzi shengpang duyin biancha* (A handy look up for the pronunciation of phonetics in Chinese characters). Jilin: Jilin Remnin Chubanshe.
[周 有光, 1980, <汉字声旁读音便查>, 吉林: 吉林人民出版社.]

www.ingramcontent.com/pod-product-compliance
Lightning Source LLC
LaVergne TN
LVHW010453160826
845677LV00012B/2469

* 9 7 9 8 5 9 1 5 2 3 8 7 9 *